Unique Artworks
COLORING BOOK
VOLUME I

SYLVIE'S INSPIRATIONS

S.C.MORDAN

The Artist

S.C. Mordan (S.C.M.) is a vibrant artist from Pawtucket, RI. An assignment from his graduate studies where he was challenged "to create anything imaginable to demonstrate creativity," altered his life. He painted his first acrylic painting titled *"Novo"* to illustrate the context of his life in order to complete the assignment. S.C.M.'s sole purpose for painting is to communicate his sentiments to the universe on canvas.

Artist Statement

I started to paint to express my creativity. My paintings document both my development and progression as an artist. I consider a painting to be a great piece of art when the message in the painting speaks for itself.

Copyright

Unique Artworks Coloring Book Volume I:
Sylvie's Inspirations

Copyright ©2021 by S.C. Mordan All rights reserved. No part of this publication may be reproduced or transmitted in any form or by any means, including photocopy, without prior permission in writing from the artist (author) or publisher.

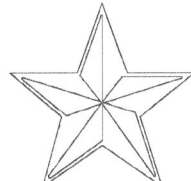 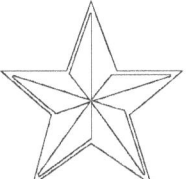

Dedication

This book is dedicated to J.S.B-M. You will always be my #1.

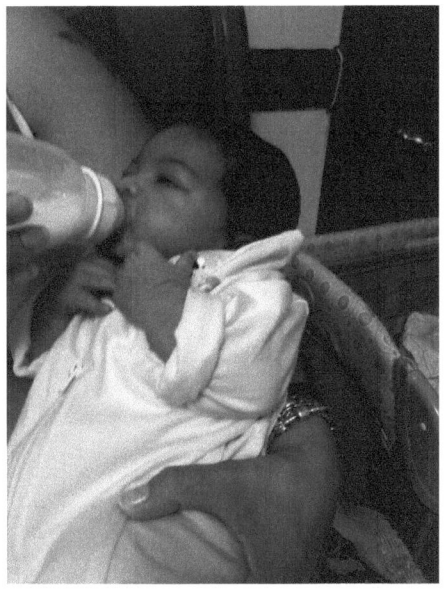

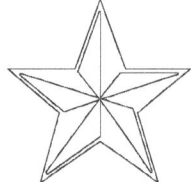
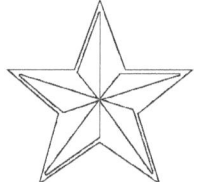

This Book Belongs To:

_____

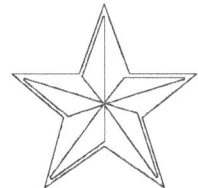 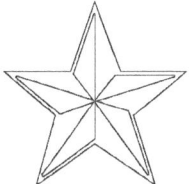

EXHIBITIONS

Some of the artworks featured in this book were exhibited at the following venues:

AS220 Gallery	RI
Warwick Public Gallery	RI
Metro Gallery	RI
Pawtucket Arts Collaborative	RI
Rhode Island Watercolor Society	RI
The Mint Gallery	RI
Pawtucket Arts Festival	RI
Atrium Gallery	RI
Sprout Gallery	RI

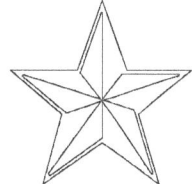 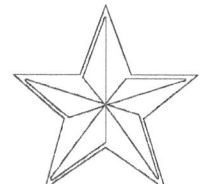

Contents

AuxRose	Black Stelo
Ignite	Blitz Stelo
Essential	Lime Stelo
Dice Trap	Cool Stelo
Engage	Warm Stelo
Six Strings	Black Trap
Chasm	Verity
Forever	Geo Tiles
Implosion	USAGlory

Instructions:

Our sketches invite you to create your own versions of our unique artworks. Use colored pencils or crayons to color in between the lines. Choose your own color variations or follow our original color schemes (see Reference page). Start coloring and unleash the artist within! Enjoy and have fun!

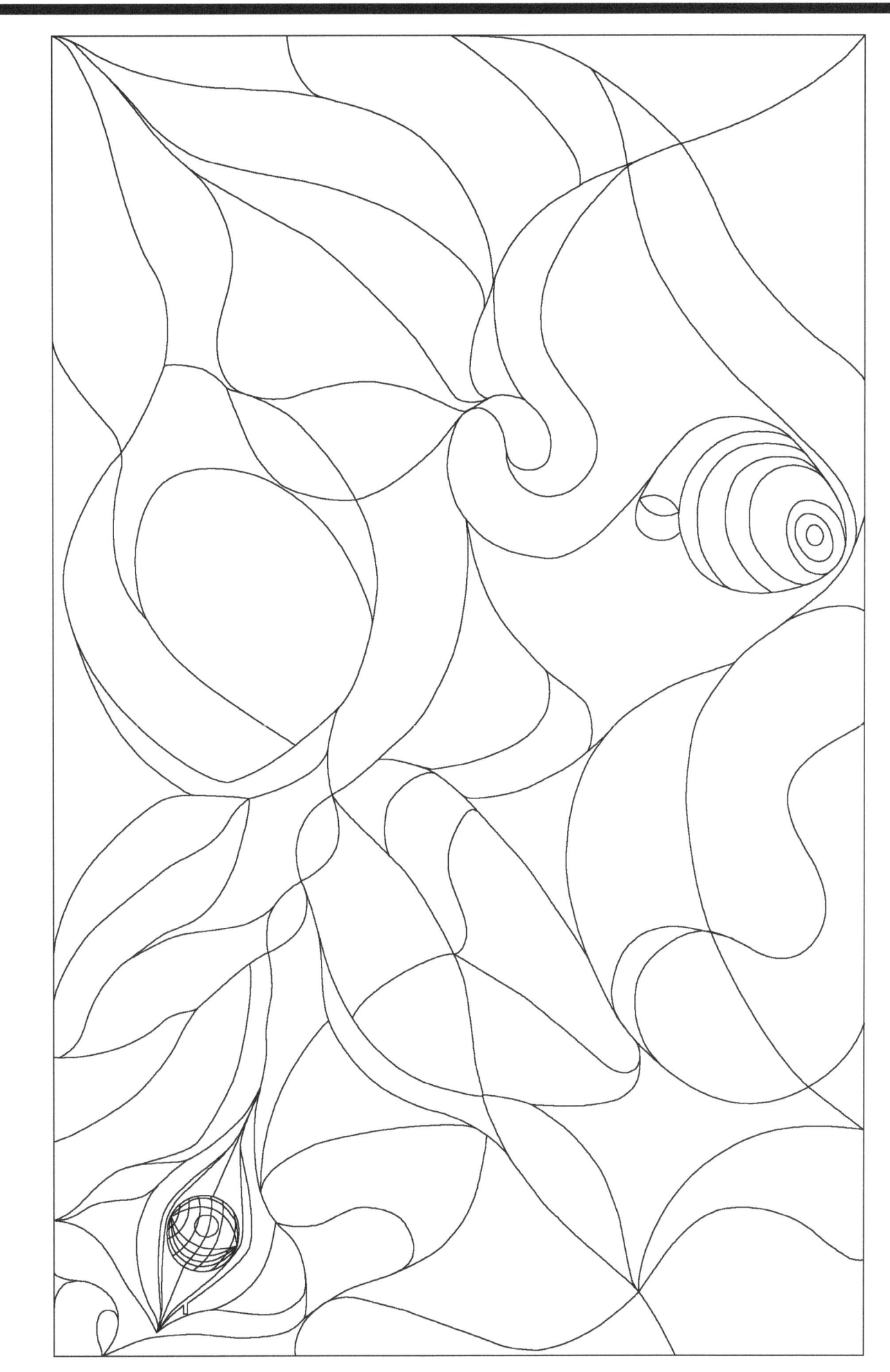

"AuxRose"   Acrylic on canvas; Size:_8"_x_10"_-Diptych (SCM2017)

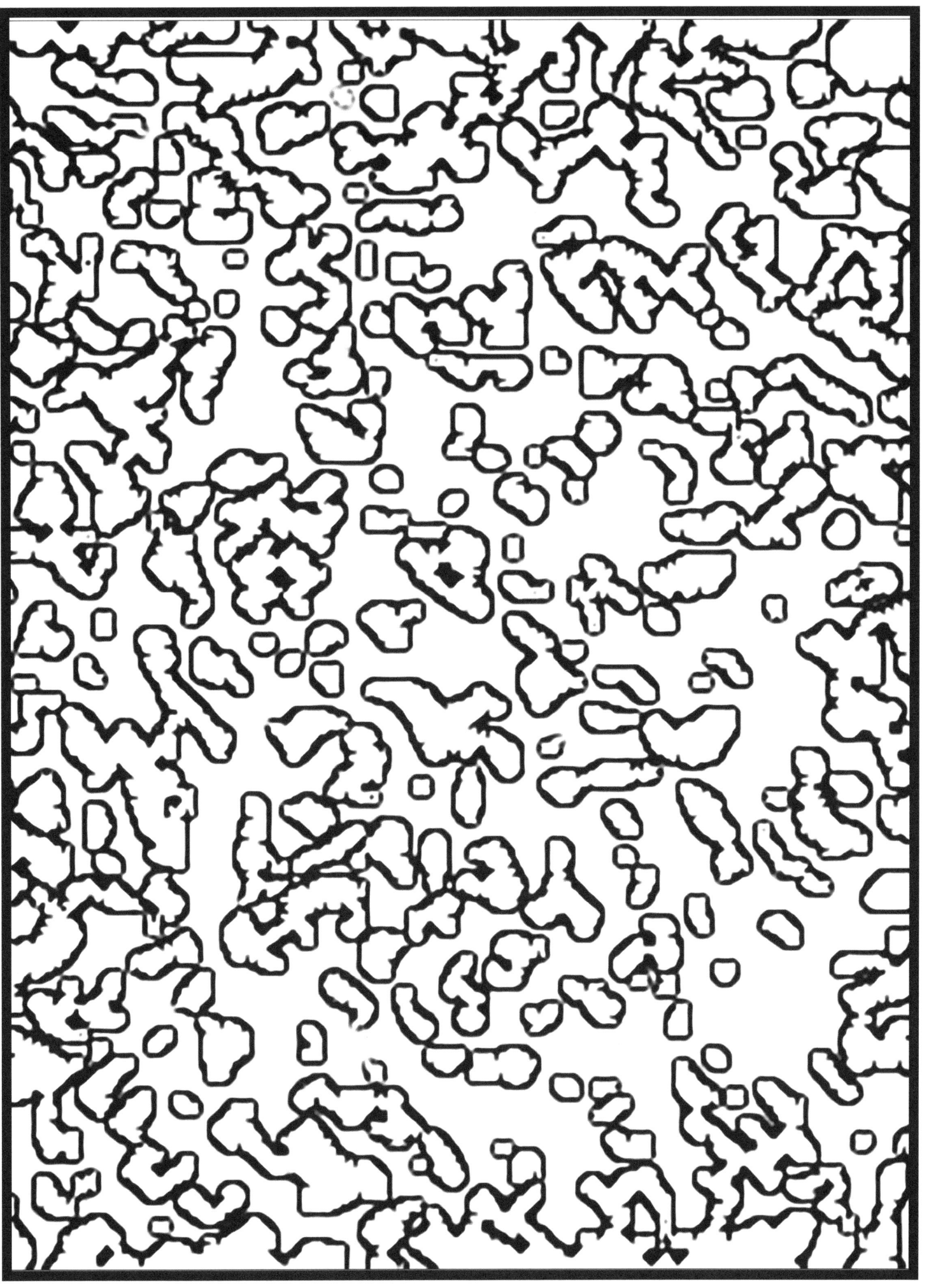

"Ignite"   Acrylic on canvas; Size:_16"_x_20"_ (SCM2014)

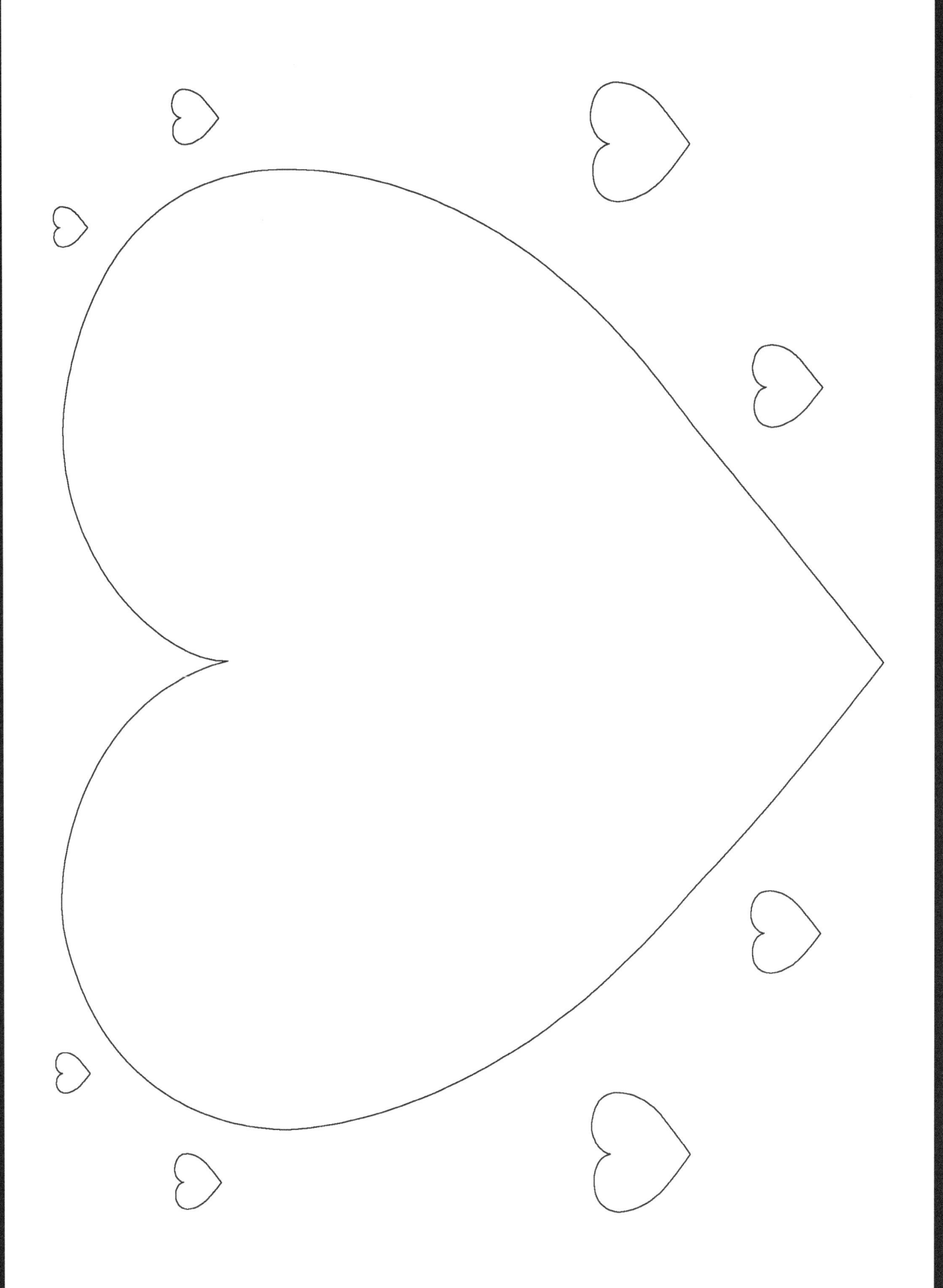

"Essential"   Acrylic on canvas; Size:_18"_x_24"_ (SCM2014)

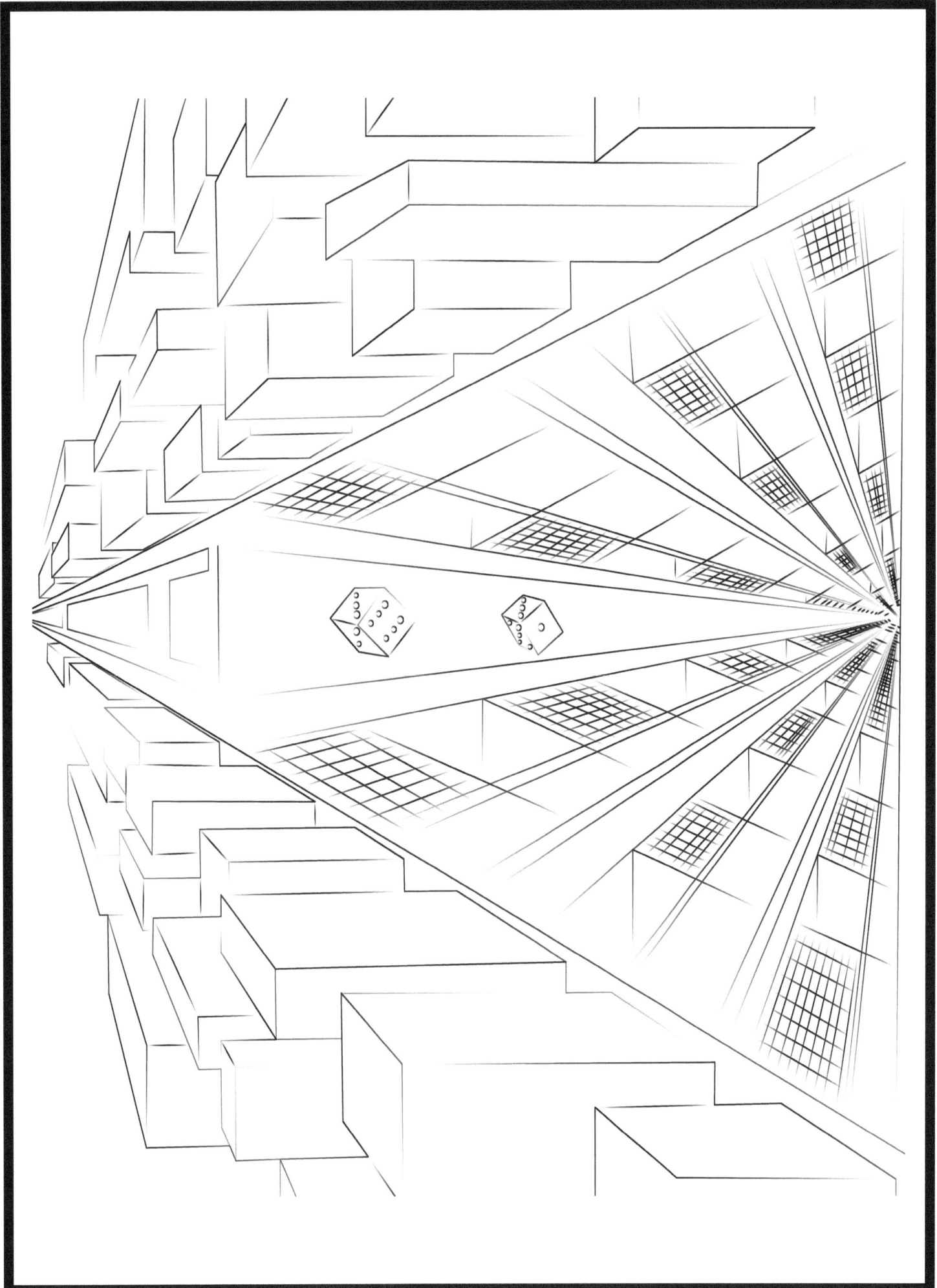

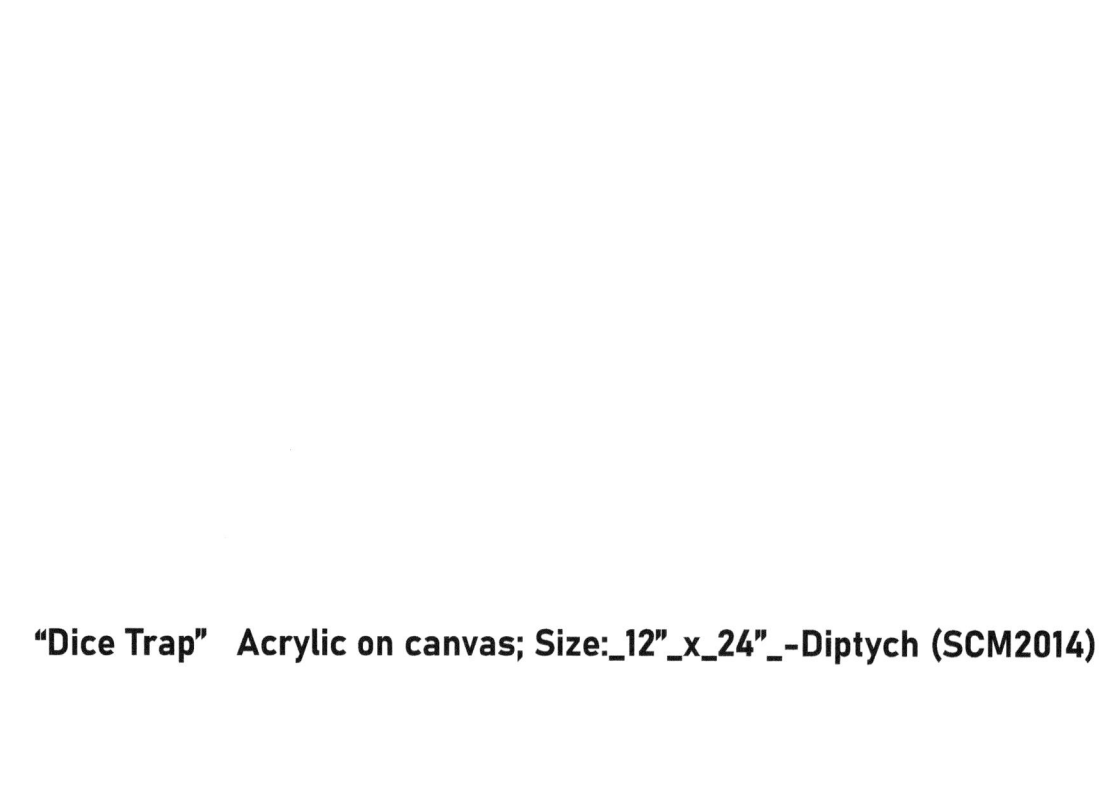

"Dice Trap"   Acrylic on canvas; Size:_12"_x_24"_-Diptych (SCM2014)

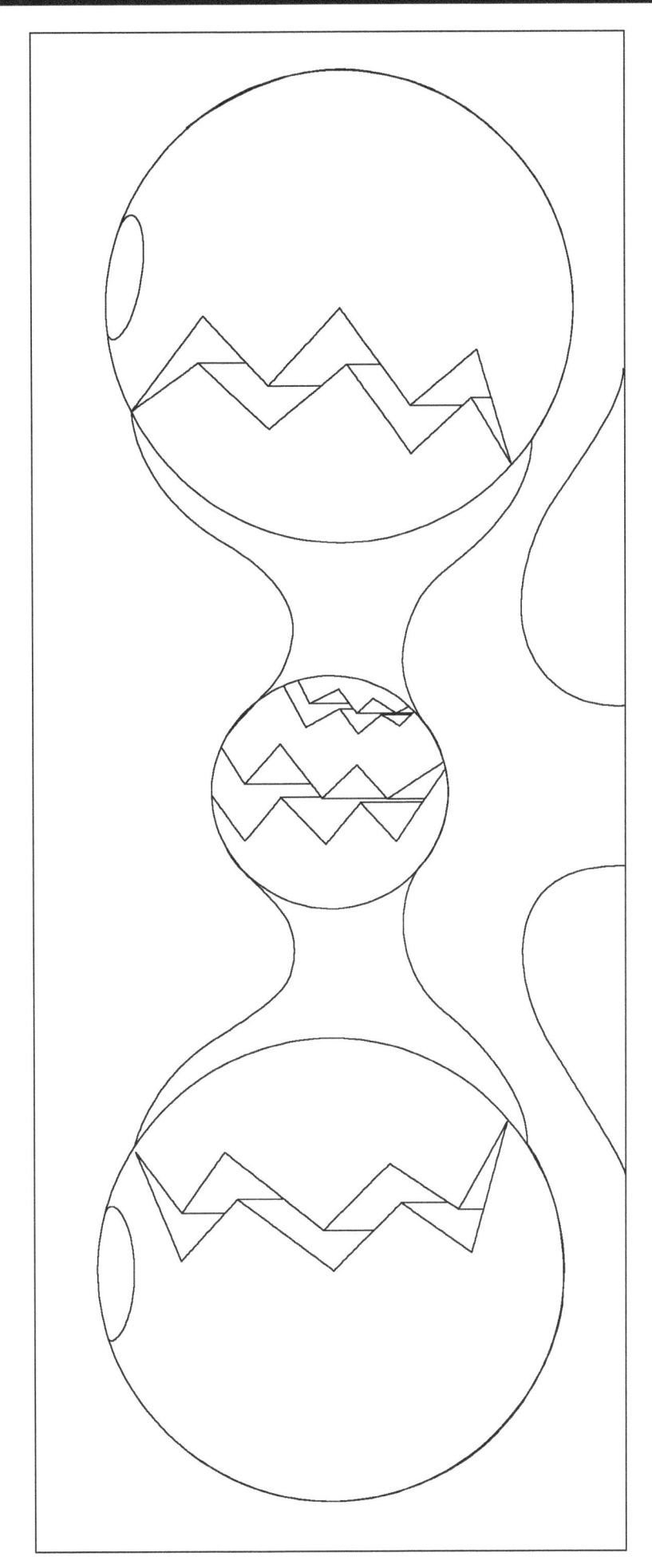

"Engage"   Acrylic on canvas; Size:_16"_x_20"_-Diptych (SCM2016)

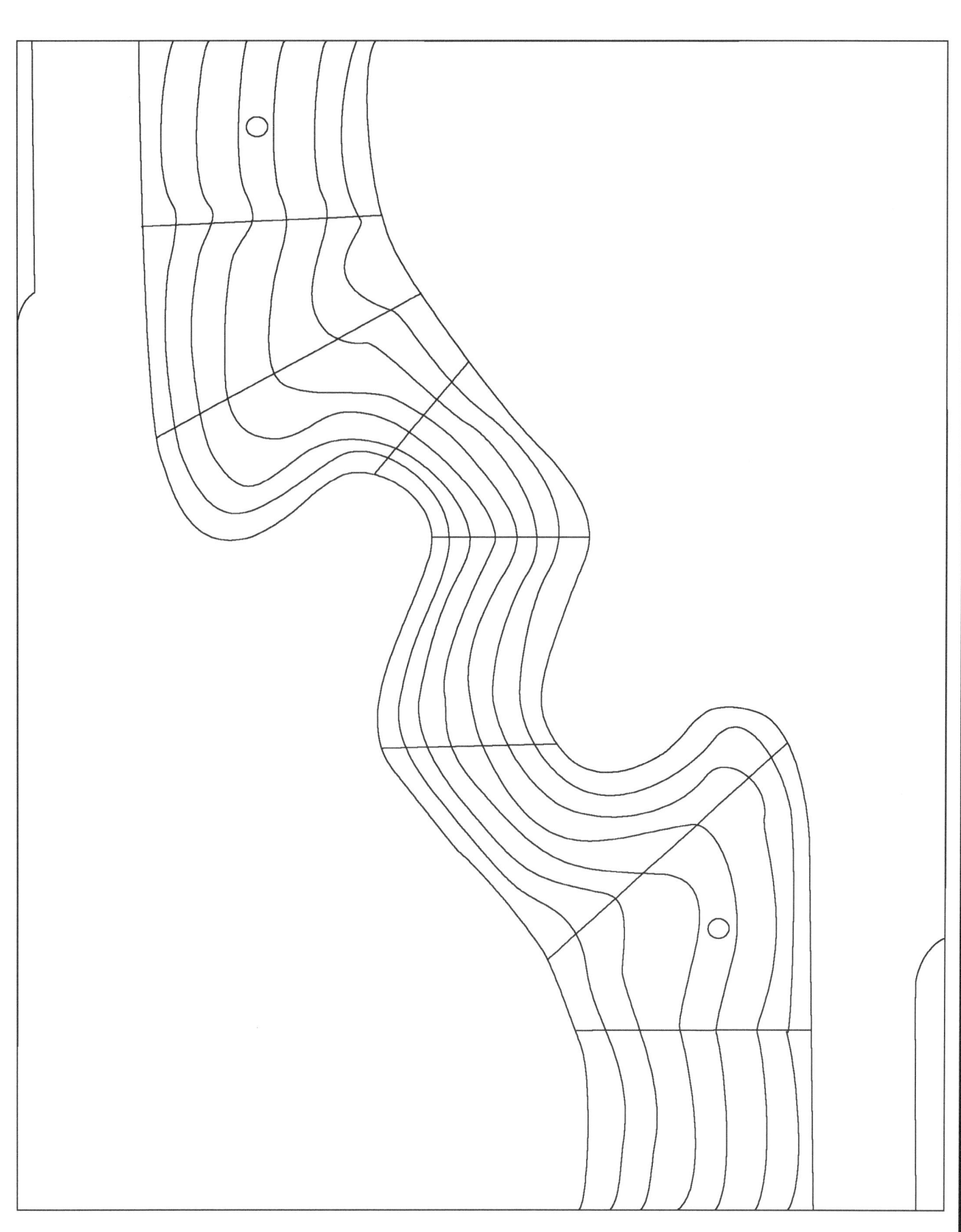

"Six Strings"   Acrylic on canvas; Size:_16"_x_20"_ (SCM2015)

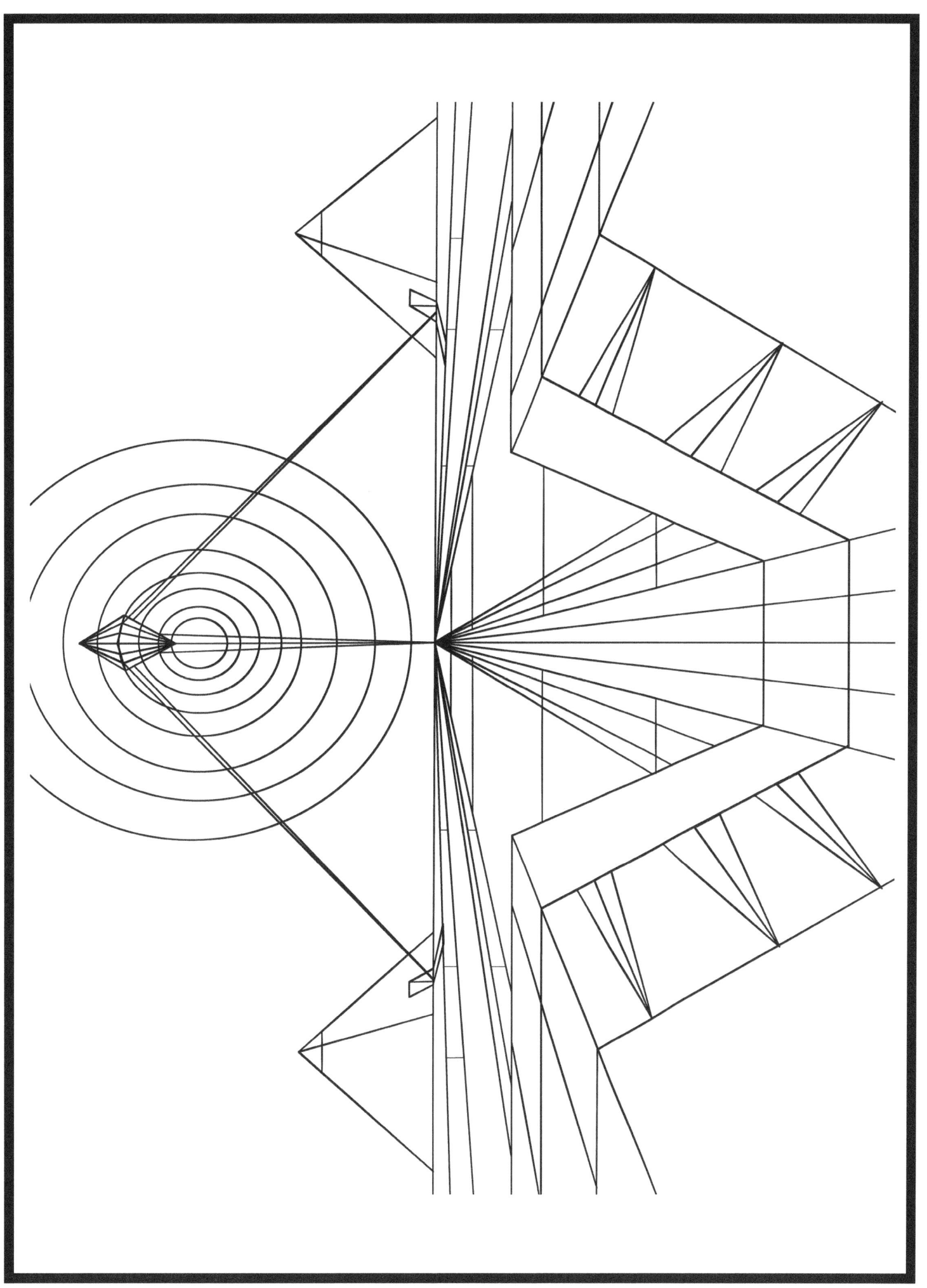

"Chasm"　Digital Art (SCM2016)

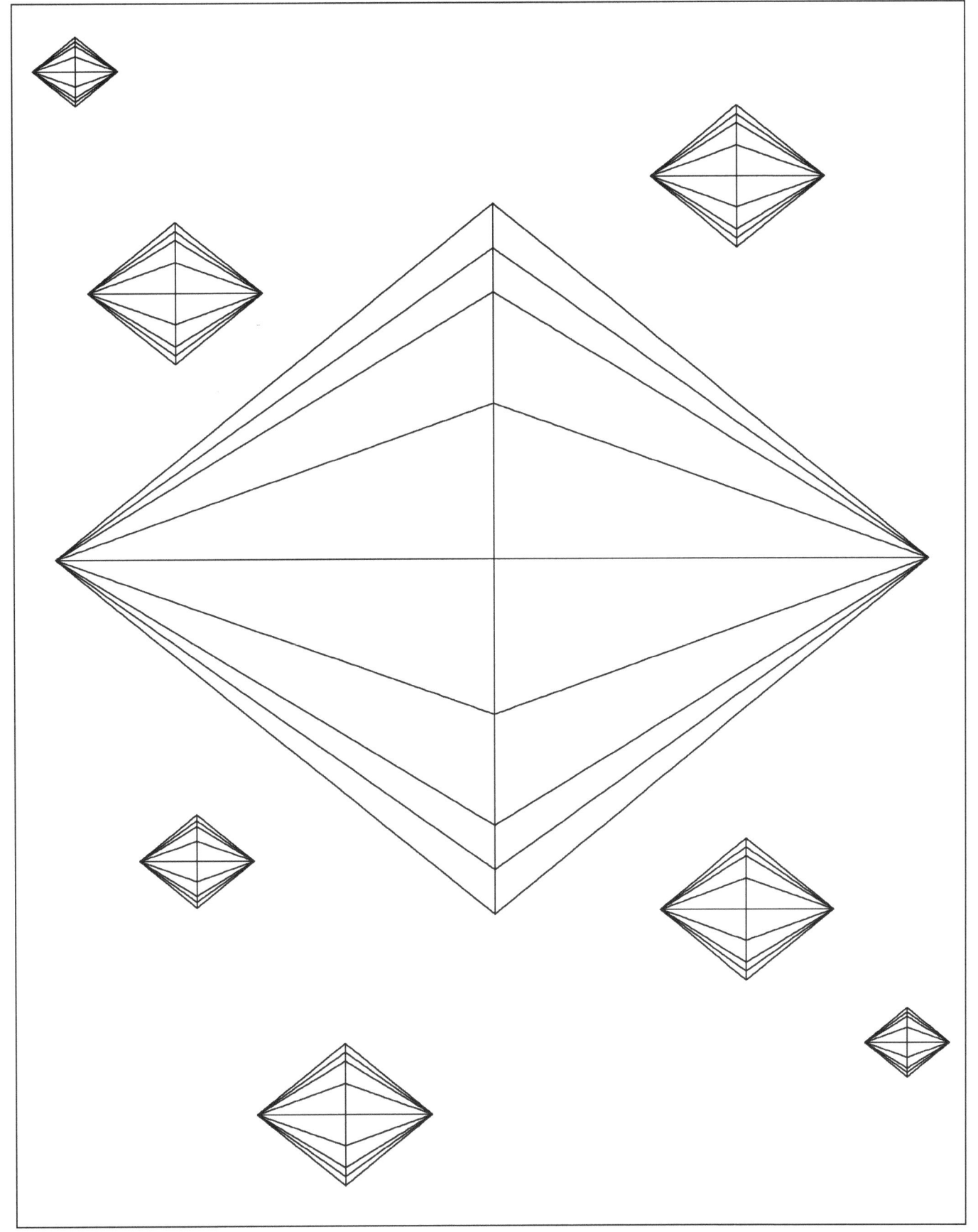

"Forever" Acrylic on canvas; Size:_18"_x_24"_ (SCM2016) *Original Not For Sale*

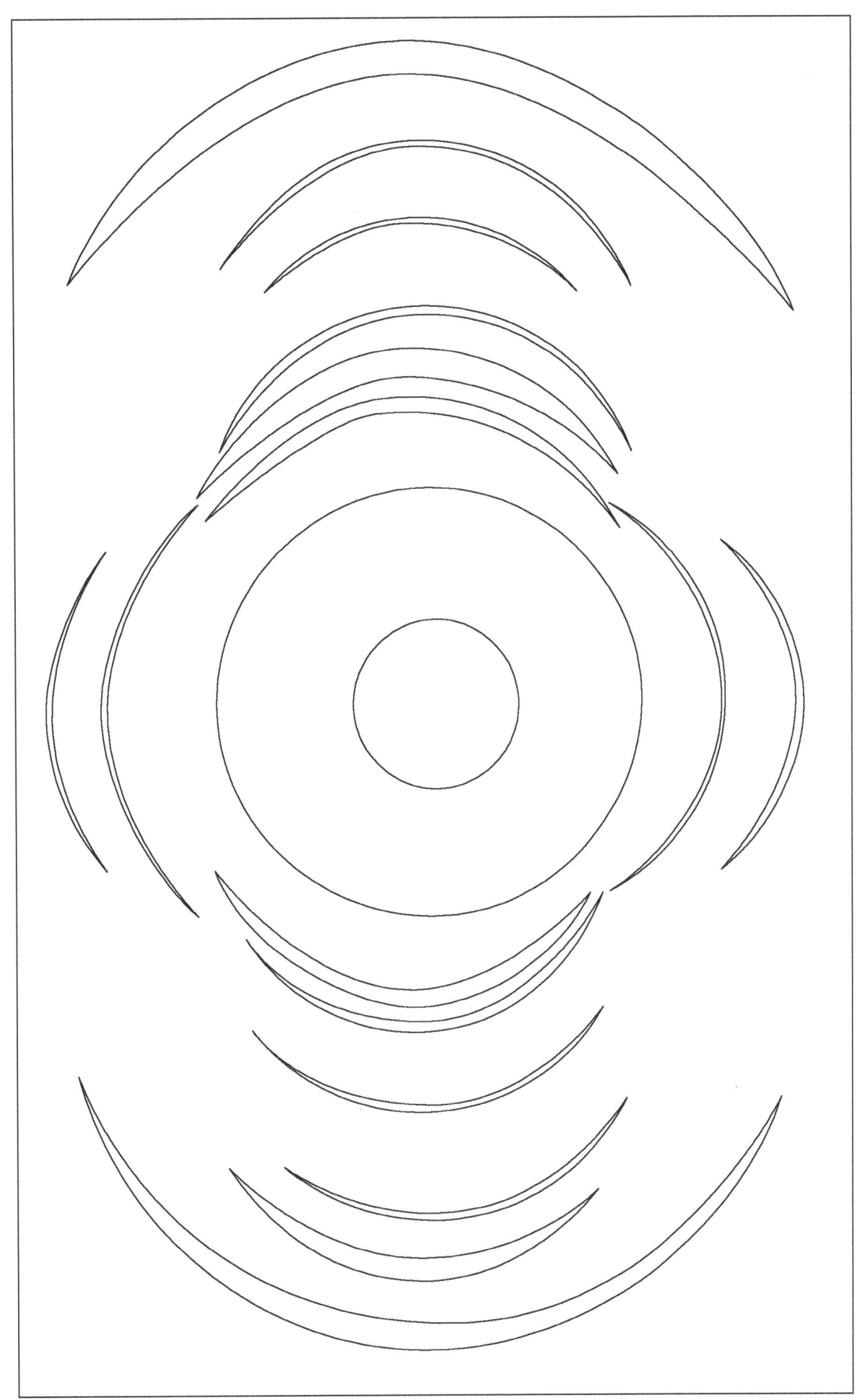

"Implosion"   Acrylic on canvas; Size:_16"_x_20"_-Diptych (SCM2015)

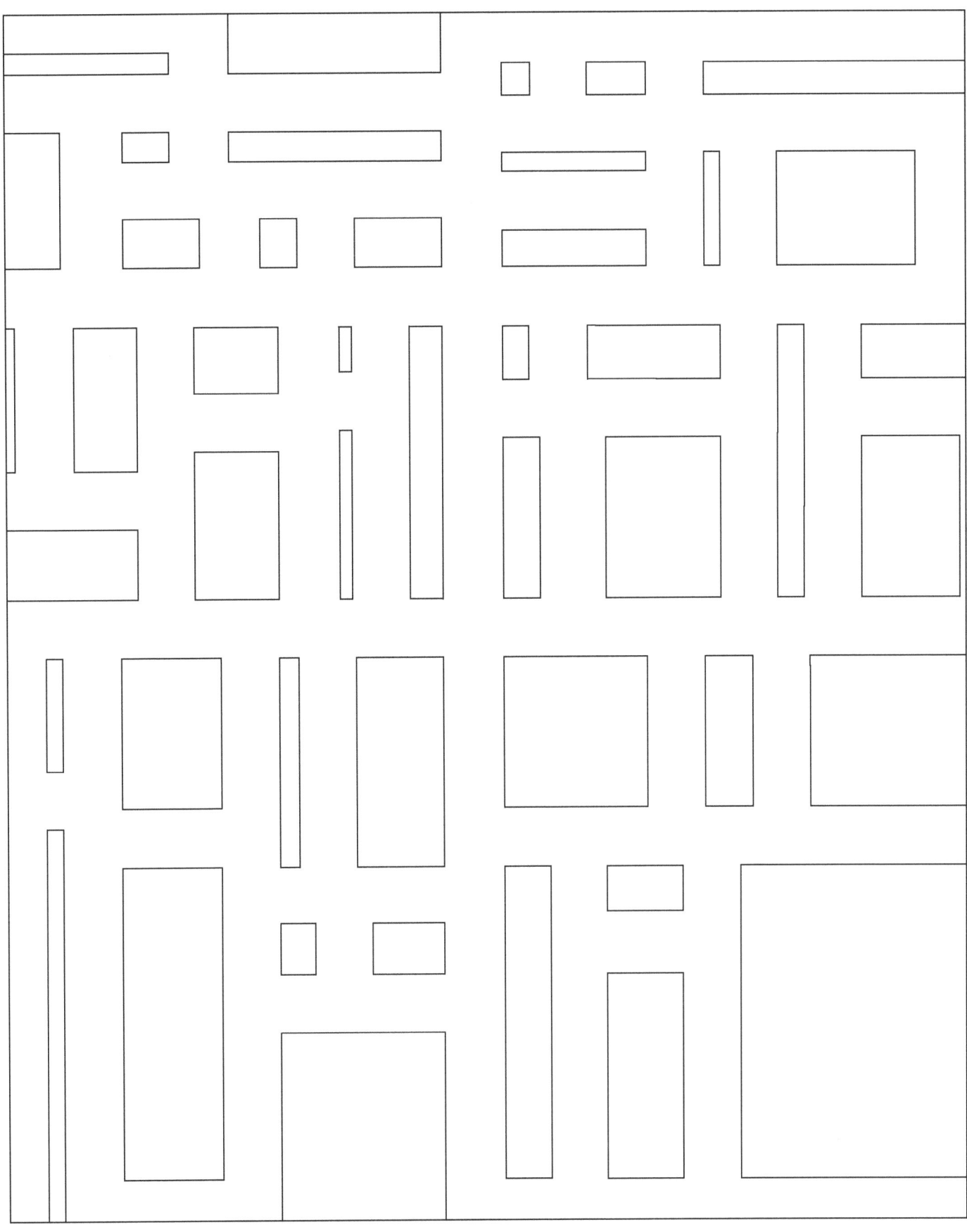

"Black Stelo"   Acrylic on canvas; Size:_16"_x_20"_ (SCM2015)

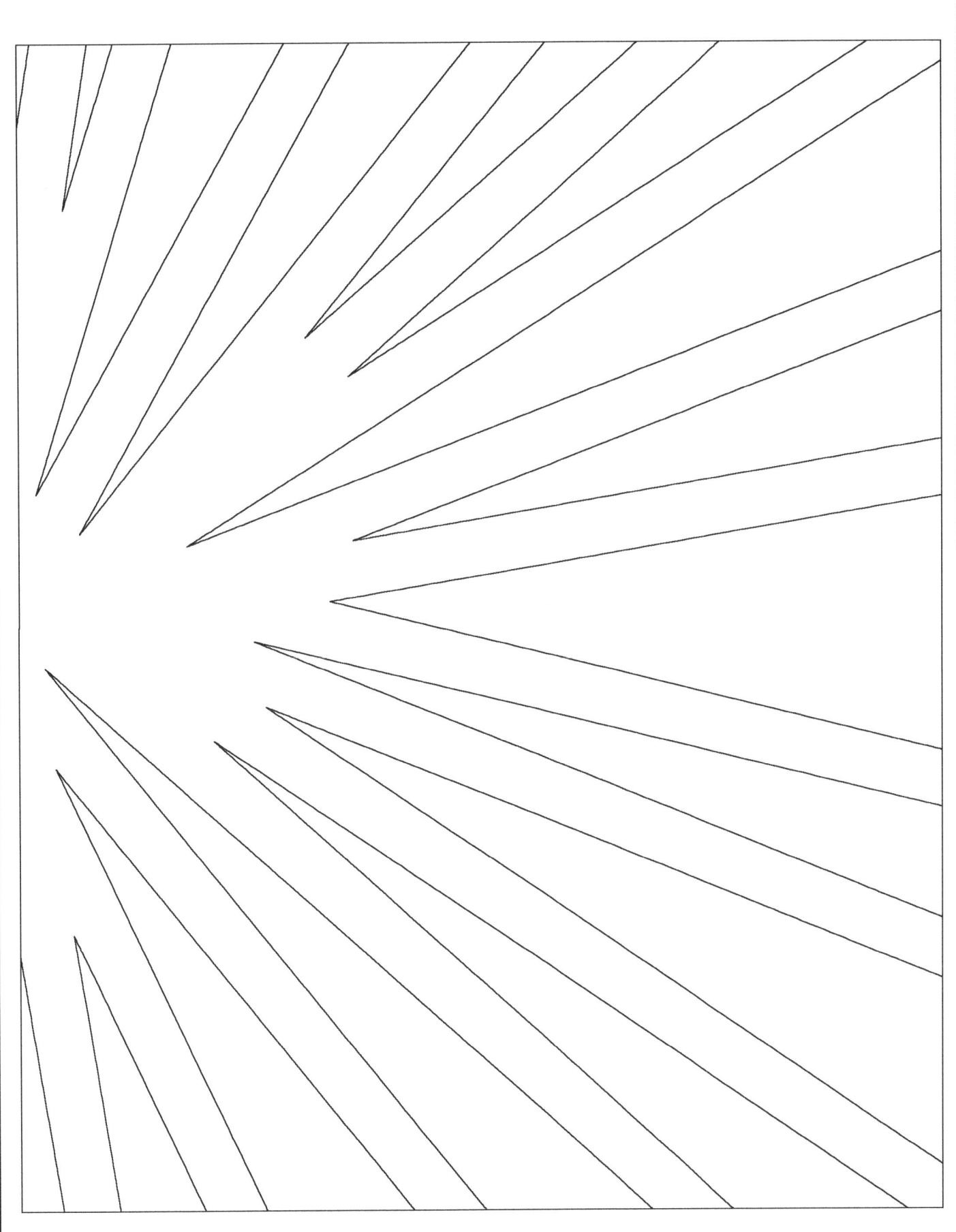

"Blitz Stelo"   Acrylic on canvas; Size:_16"_x_20"_ (SCM2015)

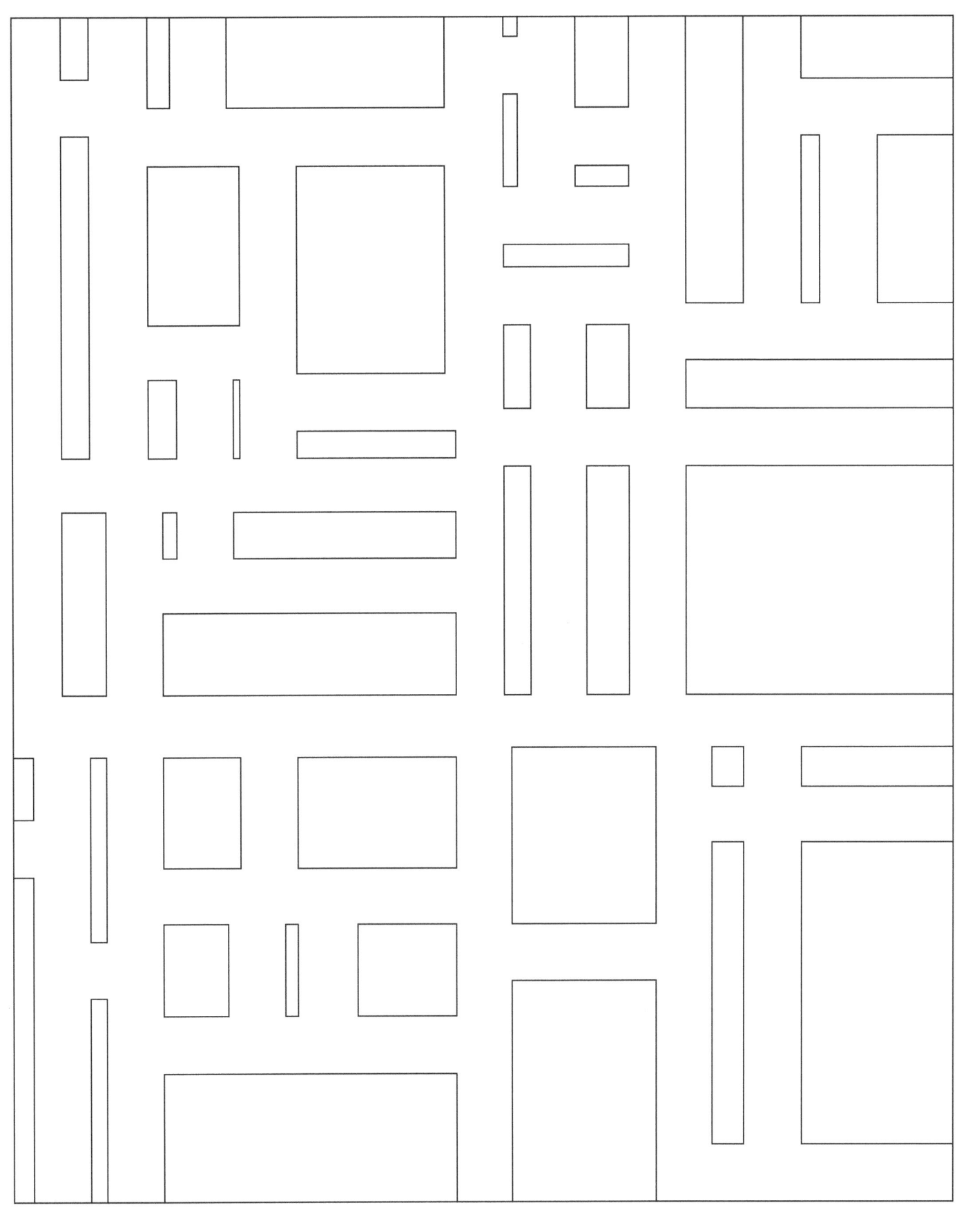

"Lime Stelo"   Acrylic on canvas; Size:_16"_x_20"_ (SCM2015)

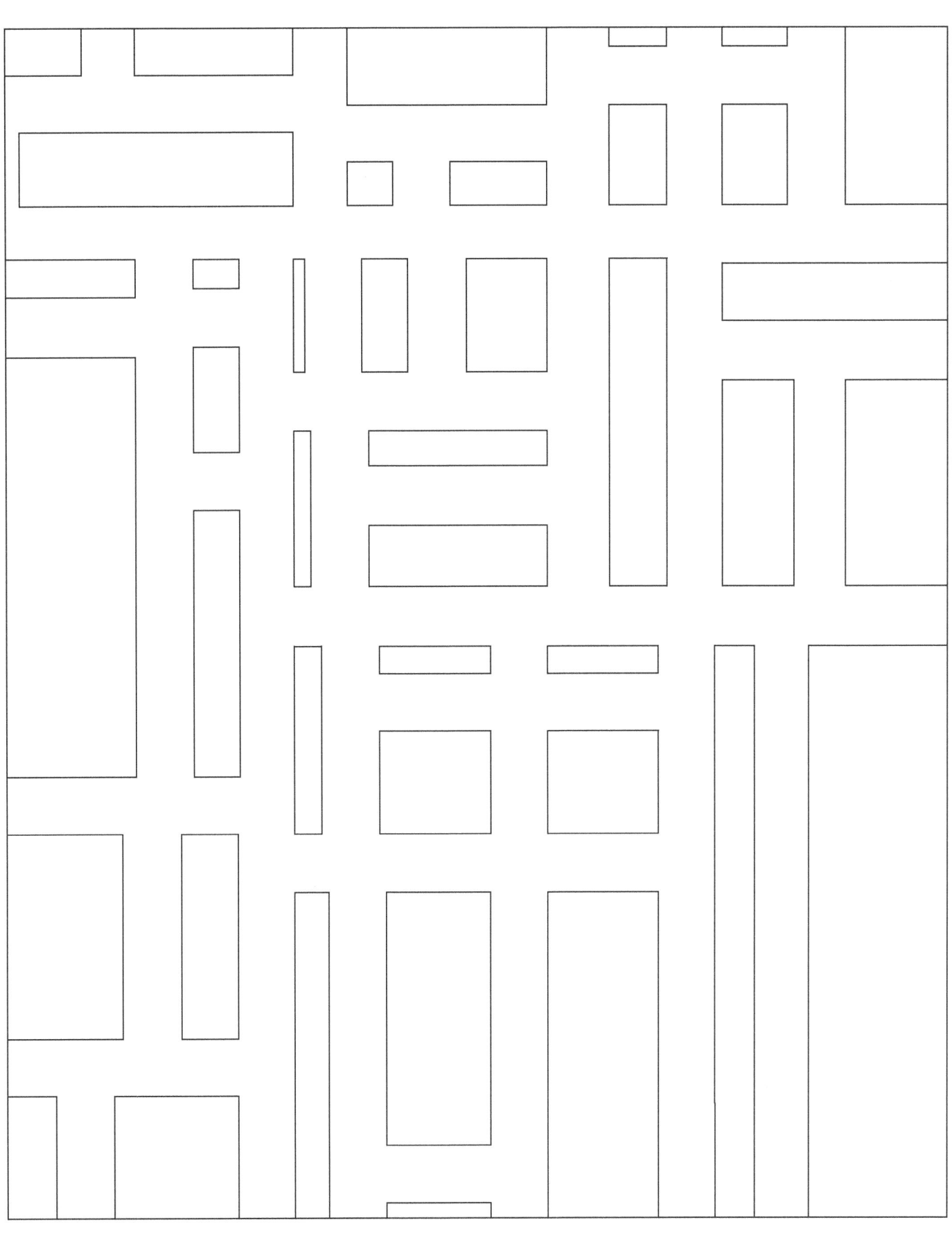

"Cool Stelo"   Acrylic on canvas; Size:_16"_x_20"_ (SCM2015)

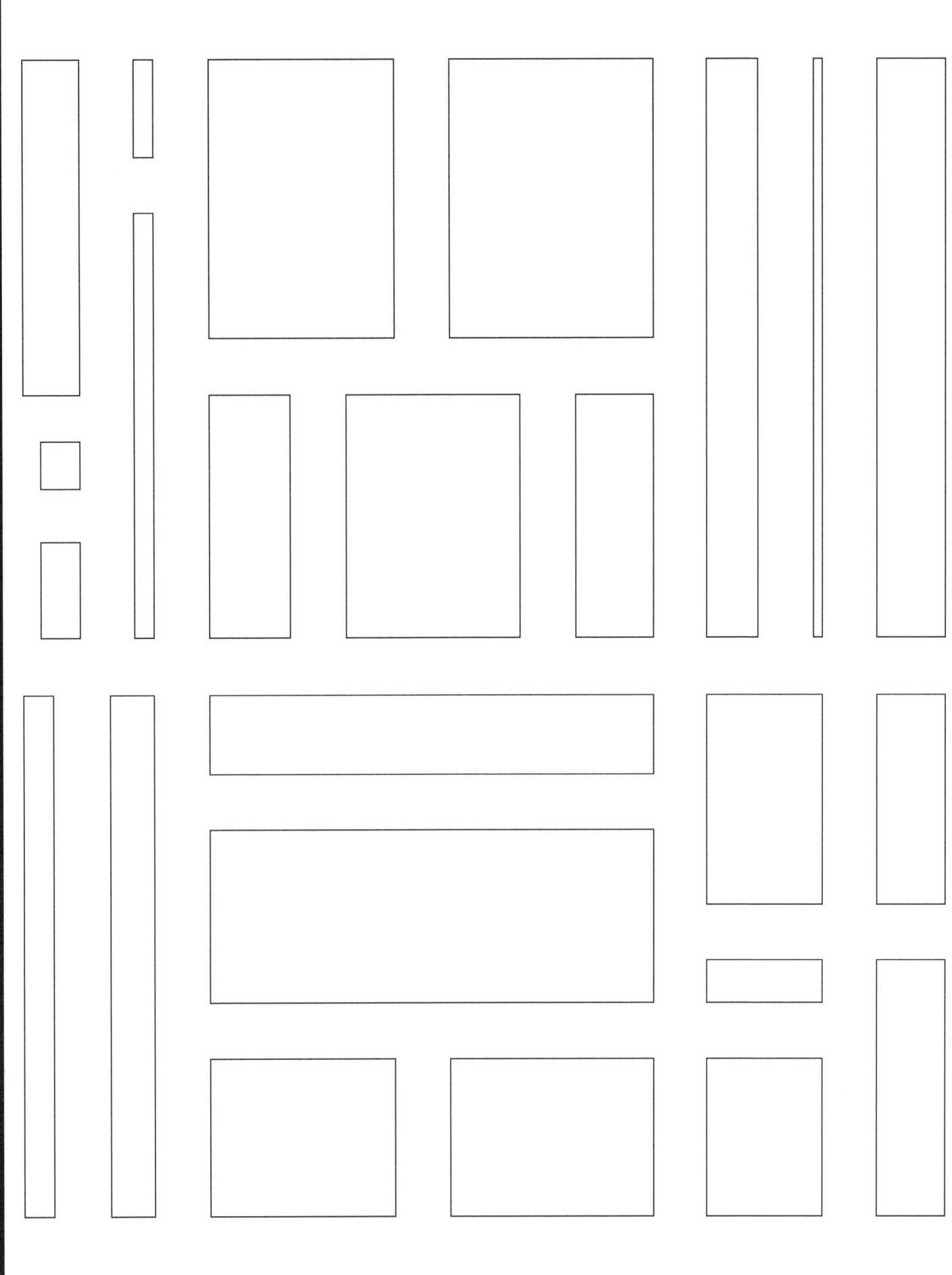

"Warm Stelo"   Acrylic on canvas; Size:_16"_x_20"_ (SCM2015)

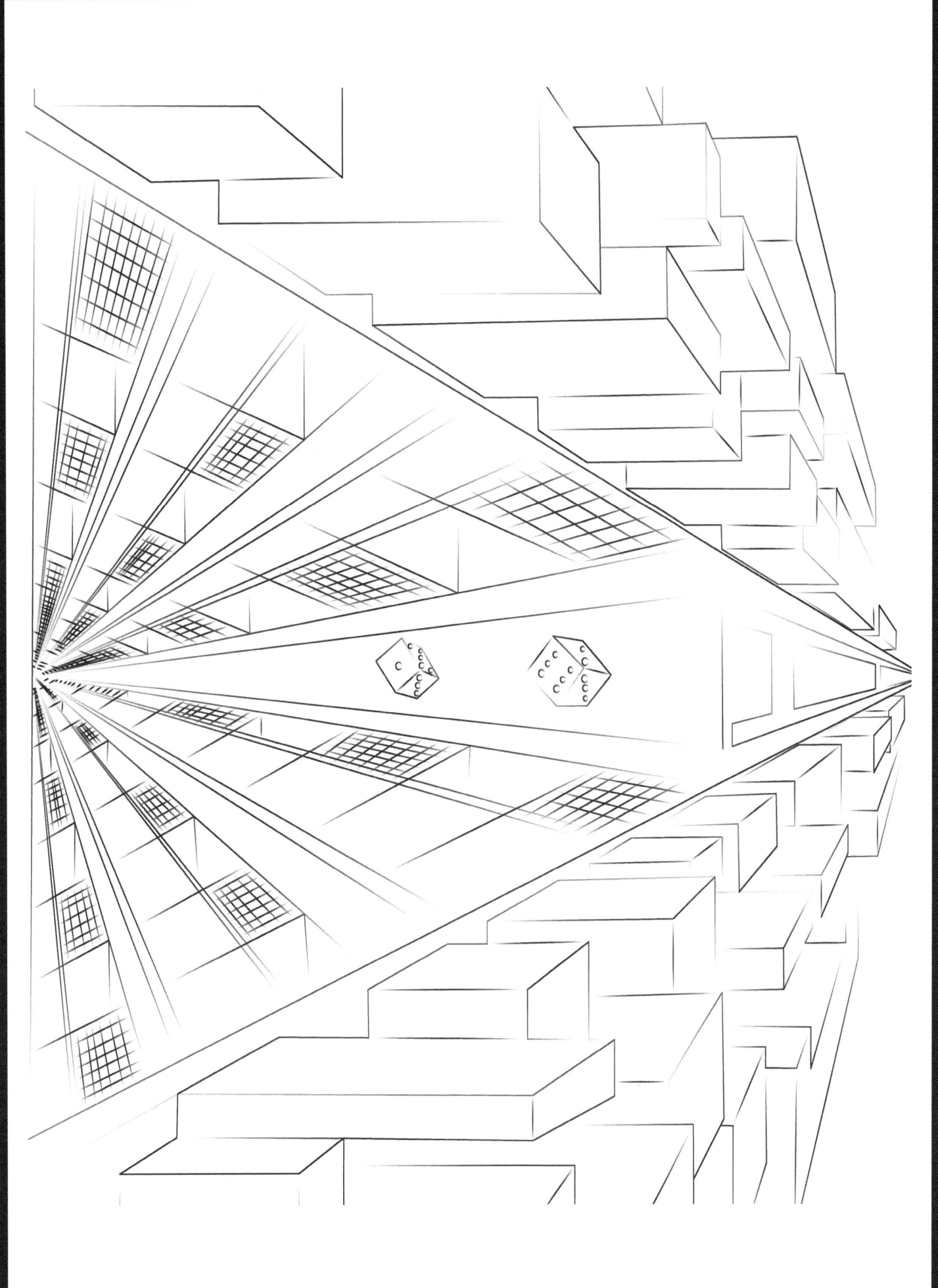

"Black Trap"   Acrylic on canvas; Size:_12"_x_24"_-Diptych (SCM2014)

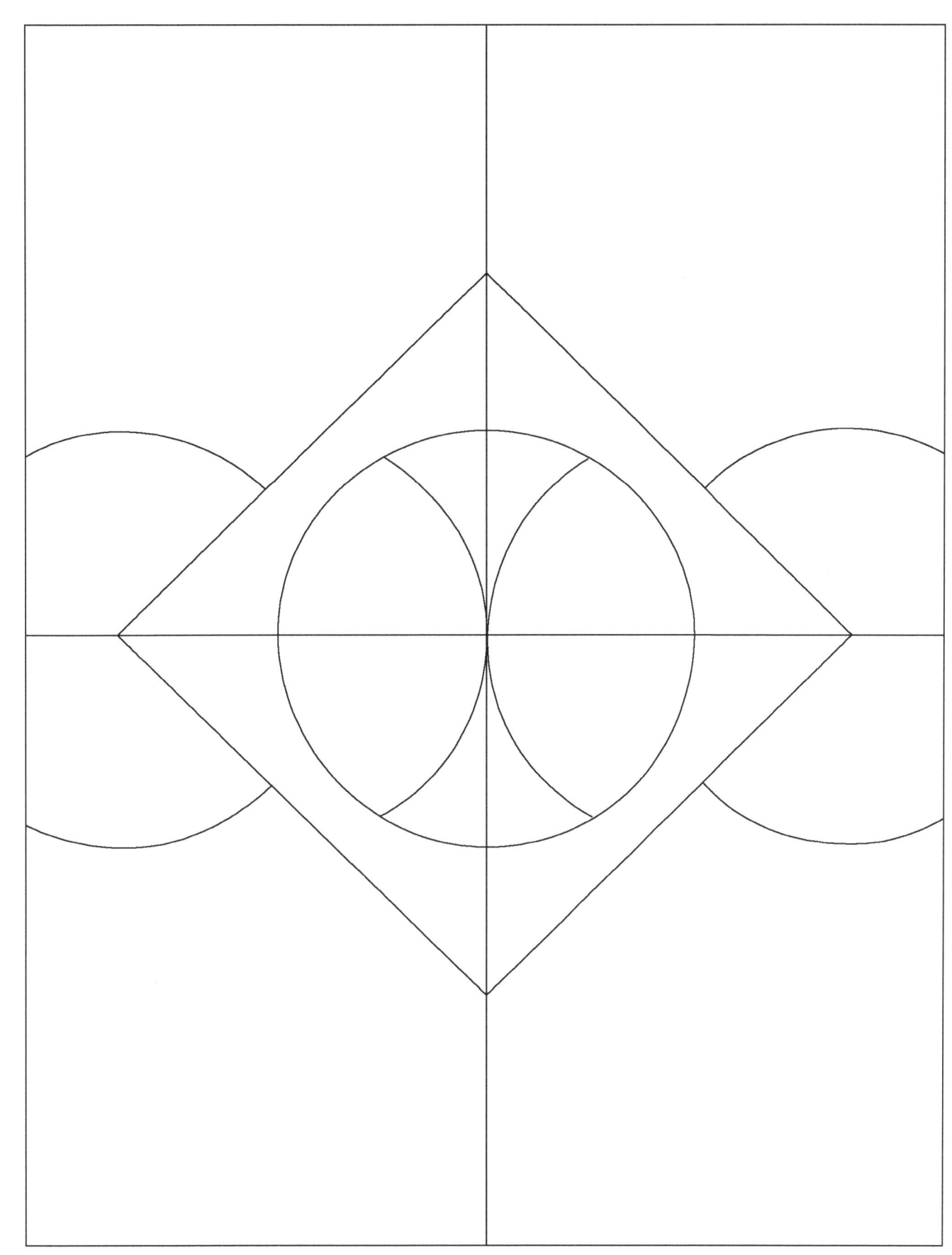

"Verity"   Acrylic on canvas; Size:_18"_x_24"_ (SCM2016)

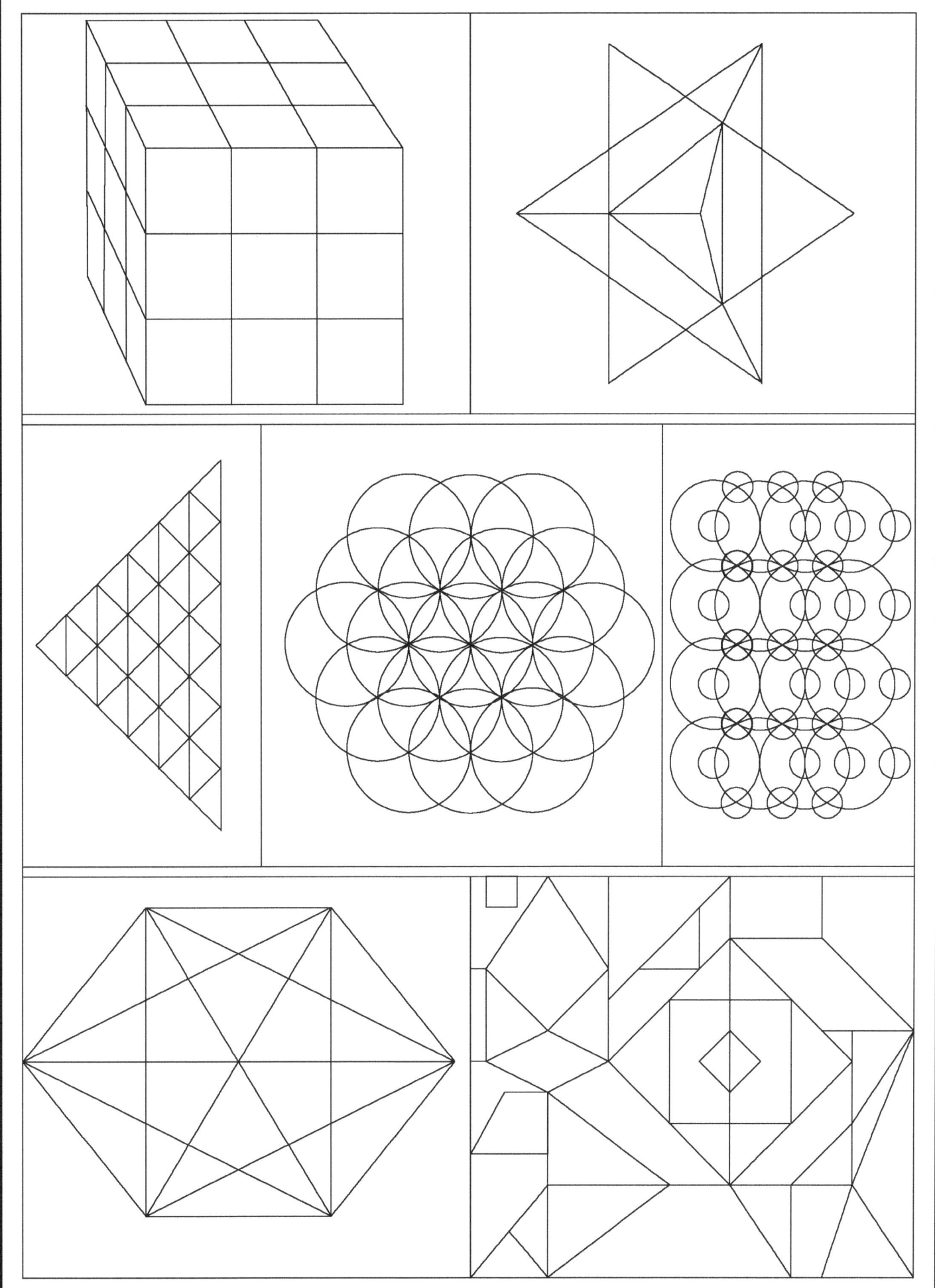

"Geo Tiles" Digital Art (SCM2021)

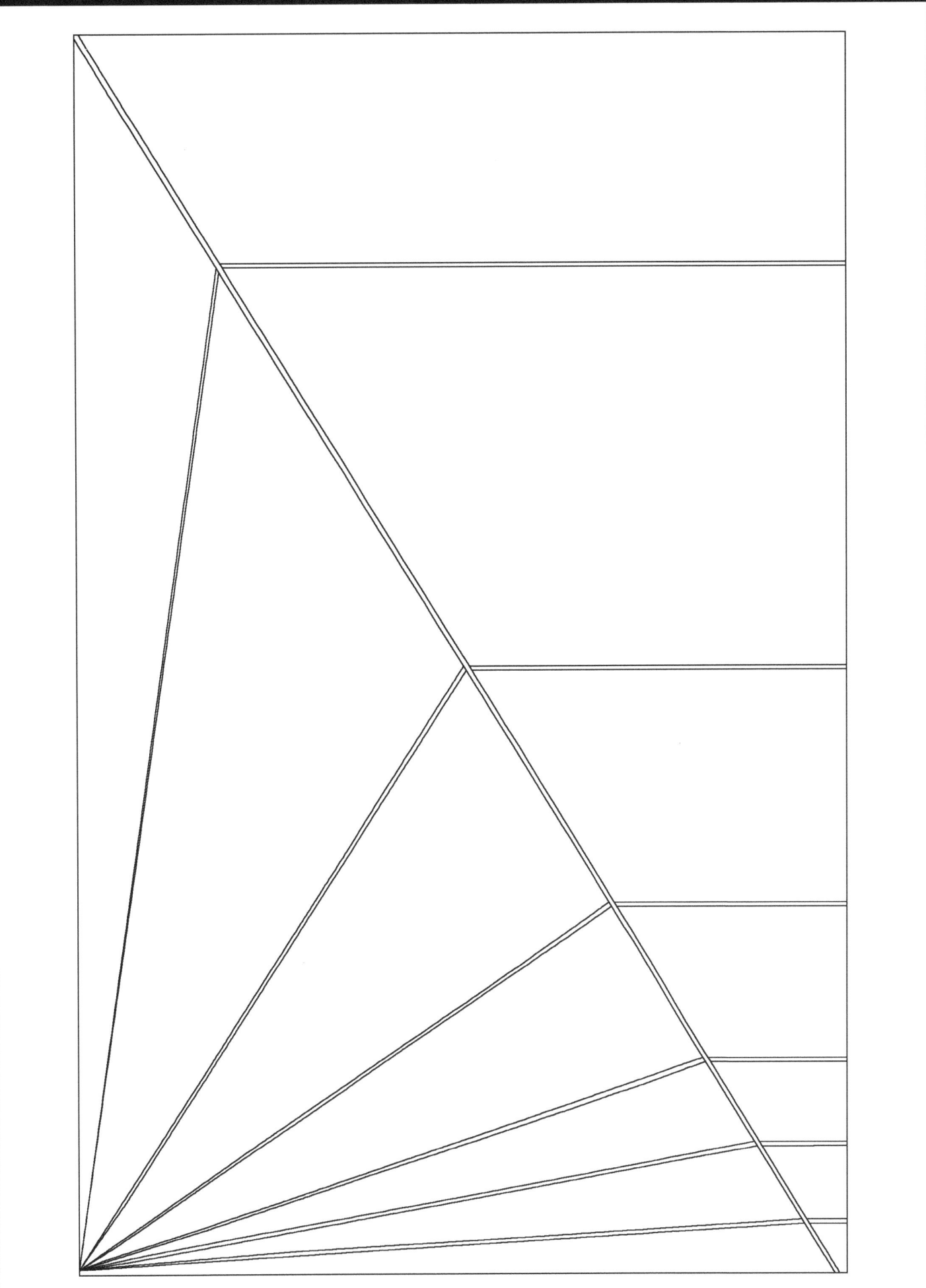

"USAGlory"   Acrylic on canvas; Size:_8"_x_10"_-Diptych (SCM2017)

Art Reference

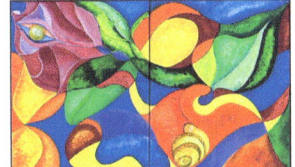
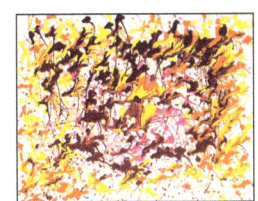
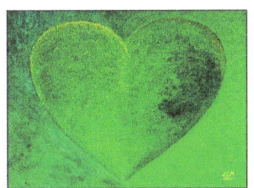
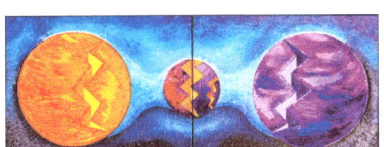
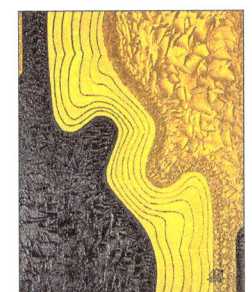
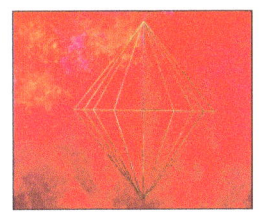
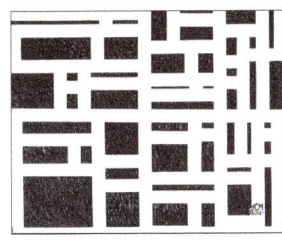
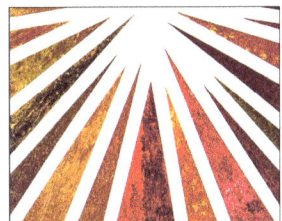
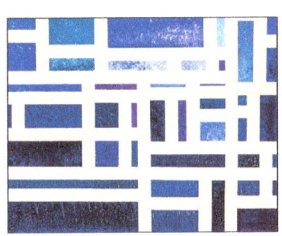
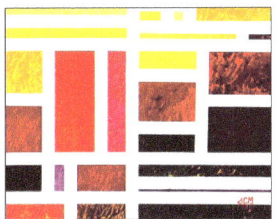
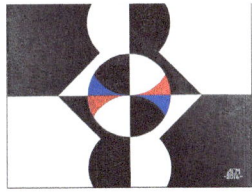
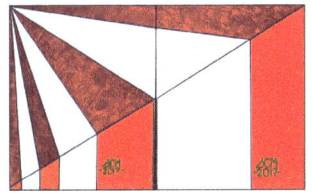

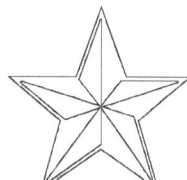
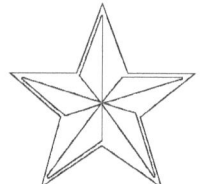

Thank You

We hope you had fun coloring our unique artwork sketches and enjoyed your artistic experience.

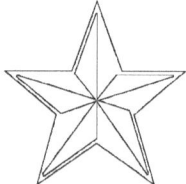
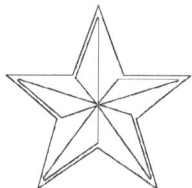

www.ingramcontent.com/pod-product-compliance
Lightning Source LLC
Chambersburg PA
CBHW040413220526
45473CB00004B/1228

9798533771382